PIPSQUEAKS!™

MAZE HALLOWEEN

Written and illustrated by Patrick Merrell

Paint

SCHOLASTIC INC.

New York   Toronto   London   Auckland   Sydney
Mexico   New Delhi   Hong Kong   Buenos Aires

ISBN 0-439-42972-2

12 11 10 9 8 7 6 5   7/0

Printed in the U.S.A.
First printing, October 2002

Halloween mazes
fill the house.
So do Pipspooks—
Eek! Frankenmouse!

Lots of surprises,
please beware.
Come and join us . . .
IF YOU DARE!

Attention, maze-solvers.
You can do all these mazes by
pointing with your finger.

EEK,
A GHOST!

EEK,
A WITCH!

EEK,
A MONSTER!

EEK,
A MOUSE!

Holy, Moly!

A haunted house
all full of holes.
To find a way
we've formed patrols.

Slowly now—
please, one and all.
One wrong step . . .
means one LO
          N
            G
              fall.

This floor could use a little fixing, couldn't it?
However, it has created a tricky maze for the Pipsqueaks.
Can you find the way across?

Cut It Out!

Pumpkin carving's
lots of fun,
but it's a mess
when you're all done.

Gobs of gooey,
gloppy guts.
Seeds and slop
all over. Nuts!

SQUIGG   SPLOT   SQUARP

What a mess, but what a maze!
Can you get through all the glop to the lit pumpkin?

Start

End

A Crepe Paper and Tape Caper

Orange crepe paper,
lots of tape,
helped to give
this maze its shape.

Up and down
the wall it goes.
Across and back
through hanging rows!

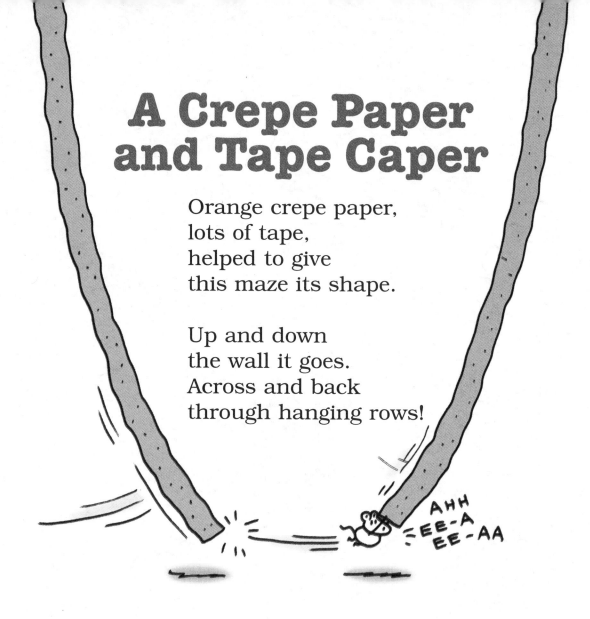

AHH
EE-A
EE-AA

The Pipsqueaks have taped a maze to the wall.
Can you find the way from "Start" to "End"?

Start

End!

Just Wing It

Bats are flying
everywhere,
in the belfry,
in our hair!

Swooping, looping,
past our hats.
Following them
can drive you . . . bats!

Can you follow the path each of these bats has taken?
Where did each one end up?

Handy
Candy

Candy corns—
a tasty maze!
Delicious paths
down yummy ways.

Please, no snacking,
hungry friends.
Or we'll be left
with all dead ends.

Quick!
Find a candy corn trail that leads to the big
pile before the Pipsqueaks nibble it all away.

Beam Scheme

Turn your flashlights
on at night.
Ah, that's better.
Aren't we bright?

Many wrong ways,
just one right.
Can you help us
see the light?

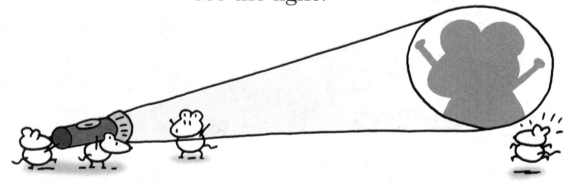

To complete this maze, you must always stay in the light.
Can you find the path that goes all the way through?

Bag It

We are going
trick-or-treating.
Soon the goodies
we'll be eating.

Up the walk,
keep off the street.
Wait in line
to get your treat.

When the Pipsqueaks go trick-or-treating they all go together. This can create quite a backup. Can you find the line that leads to the doormat?

A Sweet Treat Feat

Tons of treats
are piled up.
We've had a taste —
we're riled up.

We want some more,
but just which way?
Show us now —
without delay!

Only one path leads to the stack of goodies.
The others lead to . . . yuck!
Help us find the right way — right away!

Slither Hither

Time for games,
prepare your snakes!
Speed . . . and glue
are all it takes.

Pipsqueaks, ready?
Take your places.
Get set and go!
Begin the races!

The Pipsqueaks' favorite Halloween game is snake-racing.
Their snake friends love it, too.
Which route will get the winning team to the finish line?

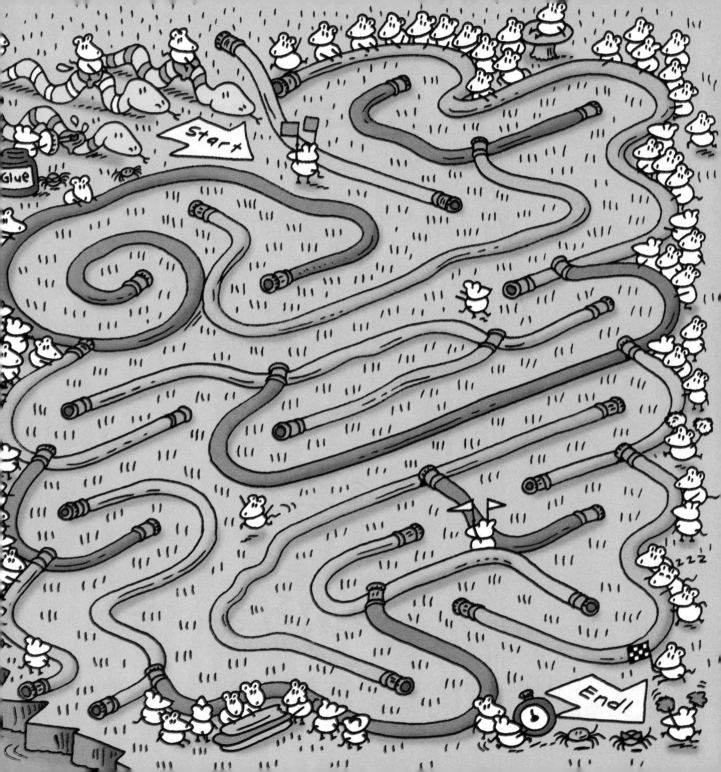

Spun Fun

As we sip
and slurp our ciders,
we try a maze made
by two spiders.

Their names, you ask?
Why, Bob and Debby!
Their maze, we found,
was quite . . . cobwebby!

Bob and Debby have done quite a good job, haven't they?
Can you find a way through the tangled web they've woven?

End!

Start

Cider

Sticky, Licky, and Tricky

Candy apples,
red and sweet.
Dip 'em, lick 'em,
what a treat!

You can make it
with some luck.
Keep on moving —
don't get stuck!

Can you follow the trail of melted red candy?

Bob Job

You will have to
gasp and grapple
with your mouth
to get an apple.

To get one out
from in the tub,
put your head in —
glub, glub, glub.

The Pipsqueaks' mouths are too small to bob for apples.
Instead, they've made — guess what — a maze with the apples.
Can you help get them across this tub?

A Maze of Days

Getting through
this monthly maze
will take us more than
thirty days!

Across the page
we slip and sneak.
From day to day
and week to week.

The Pipsqueaks have found an old calendar.
They have painted out some of the lines.
Can you find the route from the 1st to the 31st?

How to Make a HALLOWEEN CALENDAR MAZE!

Here's a fun activity to make with an old calendar.

Find an old calendar — one nobody needs. You'll also need a pencil, an eraser, and some white paint.

Find the month of October. Write "Start" on October 1st. Write "End" on October 31st.

Using your pencil, lightly draw a line that snakes around the calendar from the 1st to the 31st. Remember to include a few wrong turns that lead to dead ends.

(**Note**: Make sure your pencil line passes through the *center* of each line it crosses!)

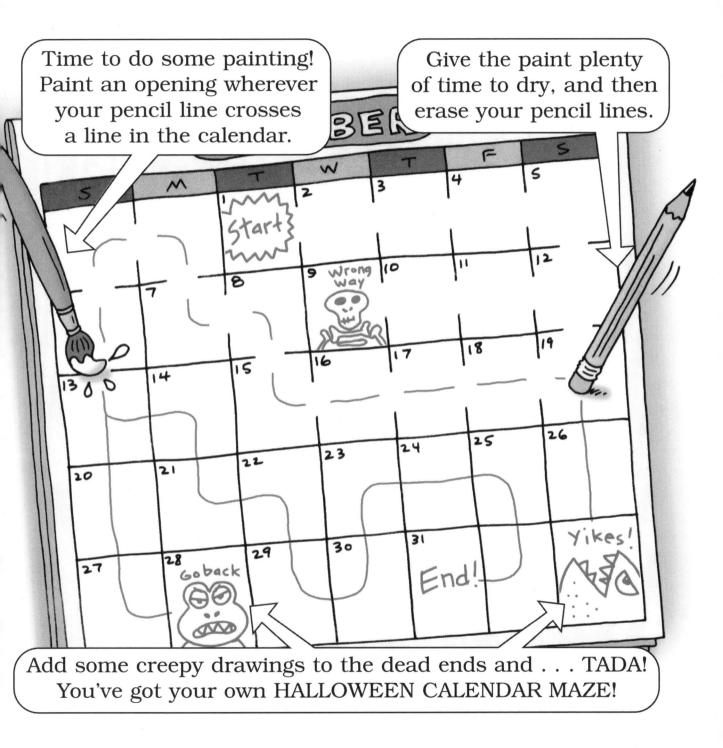

Spider Hider

You will find,
if you will gaze,
two spiders hidden
in each maze.

Where'd we hide him?
Where'd we hide her?
When you find them,
call out, "Spider!"

Our spider friends,
Bob and Debby,
are hiding in every maze.
Can you find each pair?